U.S. DEPARTMENT of the TREASURY
CDFI FUND
Community Development Financial Institutions Fund

ONE YEAR AT A TIME

Fiscal Year 2012

BUILDING STRONGER COMMUNITIES TOGETHER

CDFI FUND
YEAR IN REVIEW

TABLE OF CONTENTS

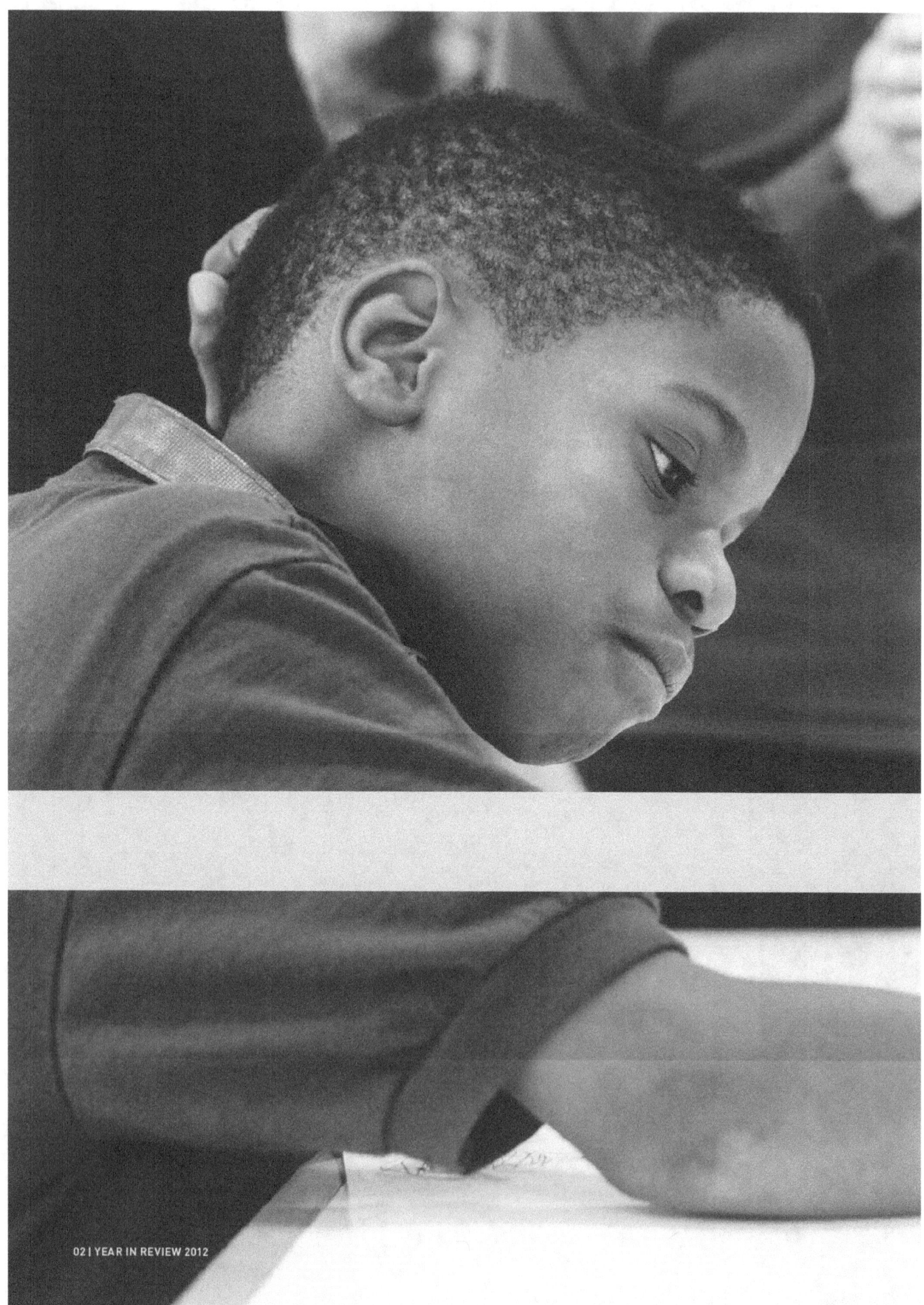

INTRODUCTION AND OVERVIEW

ONE YEAR

A Message from Director Donna J. Gambrell

CDFI FUND'S
VISION AND MISSION

The CDFI Fund's vision is to economically empower America's underserved and distressed communities. Its mission is to increase economic opportunity and promote community development investments for underserved populations and in distressed communities in the United States.

Dear Friends:

I am proud to have a new publication to showcase both the accomplishments of the staff and the programs at the CDFI Fund, as well as the tremendous impact that Community Development Financial Institutions (CDFIs) and Community Development Entities are having across the country. This "2012 Year in Review" has been designed to emphasize the CDFI Fund's continuing commitment to building the CDFI industry and spurring economic growth within distressed communities.

In times of economic uncertainty, we frequently rely upon the familiar adage "do more with less," a saying with which I am sure many of our CDFIs are familiar. The consistently high demand for the CDFI Fund's programs illustrates how CDFIs utilize all possible options available to them to meet the need for innovative financial solutions in their communities, to strengthen themselves as institutions, and to expand their services in an attempt to reach as many low-income customers as possible.

While the economy is improving, it is still difficult for many Americans and many organizations to find affordable credit, positioning CDFIs as the essential alternative to high-interest loans and payday lenders. In many cases our awards provide the essential infusion of capital that allows CDFIs to maintain their missions of serving low-income and distressed communities, and the CDFI Fund has remained ever mindful of this great responsibility of supporting CDFIs across the country.

AT A TIME

The CDFI Fund has always strived to dedicate as many resources to the CDFI industry as possible. In 2012, we had our largest award round for our flagship CDFI Program in history, while behind the scenes we were reducing our administrative costs through more affordable office space and technology solutions. And by focusing on developing new trainings for the Capacity Building Initiative, dedicating new staff to certification and compliance, and standing up the CDFI Bond Guarantee Program, we continue to expand our services for community development organizations.

But the CDFI Fund's work is about so much more than the programs and services we offer. It is about changing lives, building stronger communities, and creating economic opportunity for all Americans. A strong CDFI industry is an integral part of that equation.

This 2012 Year in Review highlights the CDFI Fund's top accomplishments and the important impact that our awardees have made to advance the mission of the CDFI Fund.

Sincerely,

[signature]

Donna J. Gambrell
Director, CDFI Fund

The CDFI Fund achieves its purpose by promoting access to capital and local economic growth through the following programs:

- Bank Enterprise Award Program

- CDFI Bond Guarantee Program

- Community Development Financial Institutions Program

- Native Initiatives

- New Markets Tax Credit Program

ONE CDFI
AT A TIME

The lack of access to financial services, affordable credit, and investment capital has long been a problem in our nation's low-income communities, and Community Development Financial Institutions (CDFIs) exist to help address that problem.

There are several different types of CDFIs, but all of them have the primary mission of serving communities and individuals that lack access to loans and other financial services from mainstream financial institutions.

TYPES OF CDFIS

Community Development Banks

Credit Unions

Loan Funds

Venture Capital Funds

CDFIs provide:

- Retail banking products and services for the unbanked and low- and moderate-income consumers;

- Loans and investments for small businesses, affordable housing projects, and social service organizations; and

- Development services, such as business planning, credit counseling, and homebuyer education, to help their borrowers use credit effectively.

The Need for CDFIs:

The gap between the mainstream financial services and low-income areas reveal the magnitude of the challenges facing the CDFI industry today. The data below demonstrates how important the work of CDFIs in low-income communities has become in the current economic environment.

For example, although more than one-third of the United States population lives in low-income areas, only 12 percent of ong-term lending (Home Mortgage Disclosure Act (HMDA) loans) and only 24 percent of Small Business Administration loans are located in low-income areas:

BENCHMARKING GAP IN FINANCIAL SERVICES[1]

Median Family Income	Population	Mainstream Lending	
		HMDA loans	SBA loans
Low and Very Low	33.0%	12.1%	24.4%
Moderate	49.9%	47.4%	56.9%
Middle	15.2%	33.5%	16.4%
High	1.8%	7.1%	2.3%

[1]CDFI Fund's Office of Financial Strategies & Research based on data from www.usaspending.gov, HMDA, and the 2000 Census.

CDFIs Fill the Gap

Access to affordable financial products and services is a staple of economically sound communities, yet at least one-quarter of United States households do not have a bank account and/or rely on costly payday lenders and check-cashing outlets. In recent years, the lack of access to capital investments for small businesses and other critical community development projects has led to increased need for alternative and reliable sources of financing. CDFIs fill these gaps by financing new businesses, building affordable housing, and supporting community-based social service organizations. CDFIs are extending lifelines to communities that have not only struggled for generations, but have had to bear even heavier burdens during the economic downturn.

The CDFI Fund supports CDFIs in their mission to serve low-income communities through its different award programs. When CDFI Fund awardees report back to the CDFI Fund on their activities, it becomes easy to demonstrate how CDFIs are stepping into the gap to serve low-income areas:

CDFI FUND PROGRAM DISTRIBUTION BY MEDIUM FAMILY INCOMES[2]

Median Family Income	Population	CDFI Fund Programs		
		CDFI Program	BEA Program	NMTC Program
Low and Very Low	33.0%	61.1%	89.5%	82.9%
Moderate	49.9%	30.2%	8.6%	13.6%
Middle	15.2%	6.9%	1.8%	3.1%
High	1.8%	1.7%	0.2%	0.4%

Chart Description: About 60% of CDFI Program awardees' loans are located in low-income areas, where 30% of households reside. Likewise, the Bank Enterprise Award Program and the New Markets Tax Credit Program are highly targeted to reach low-income areas.

[2]CDFI Fund's Office of Financial Strategies & Research based on data from the Community Investment Impact System.

Funding

Congress appropriates the CDFI Fund's budget on an annual basis, and funds can be used over two fiscal years. The budget is divided between program and administrative expenses. Program funds are used for program awards —grants, loans, deposits, equity investments, and capacity building/training contracts. Administrative funds are used to cover the costs to administer all CDFI Fund programs.

NMTC Program allocations are determined separately from the CDFI Fund's general budget, although the cost of running the NMTC Program is included in the CDFI Fund's overall administration funds.

In FY 2012, the CDFI Fund was allocated $221.0 million as follows[3]:

[3]Source: CDFI Fund FY 2012 Annual Financial Report.

FUNDING ALLOCATION (IN MILLIONS)

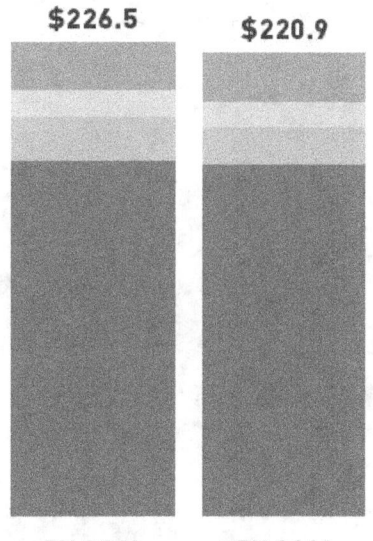

$226.5 $220.9

FY 2011   FY 2012

$22.9	Admin Costs	$22.9
$12	Native Initiatives	$12
$21.9	BEA Program	$18
$169.7	CDFI Program	$168

Note: The cost of administrating the NMTC Program is included in the total administration costs.

PROGRAM FUNDING ALLOCATION (FY 2012)

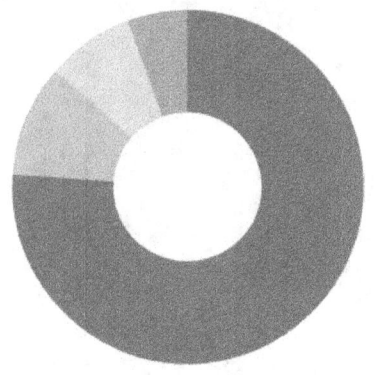

76.1% CDFI Program

10.4% Admin Costs

8.1% BEA Program

5.4% Native Initiatives

FY 2012
AT A GLANCE

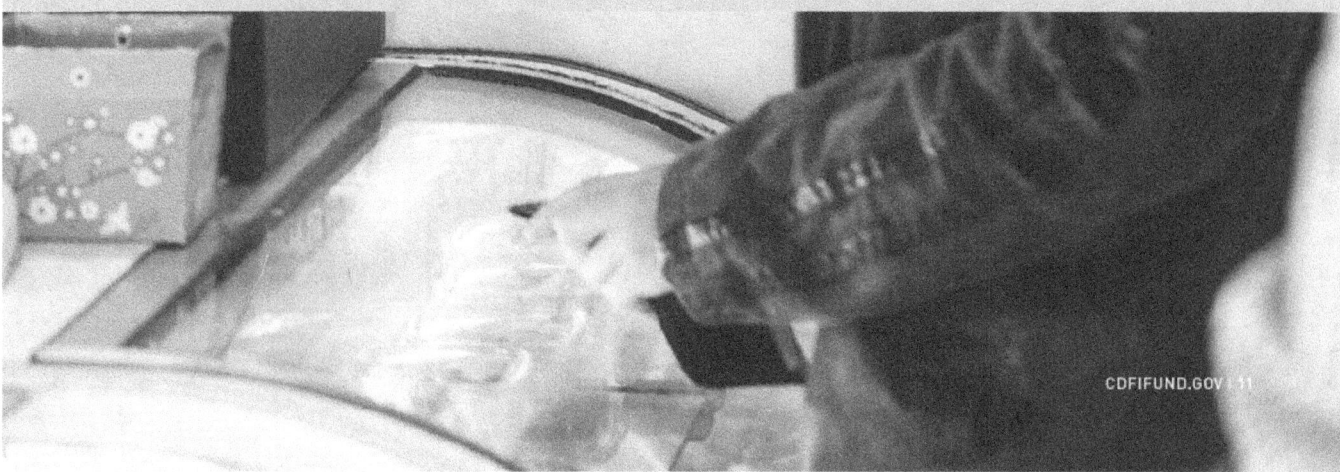

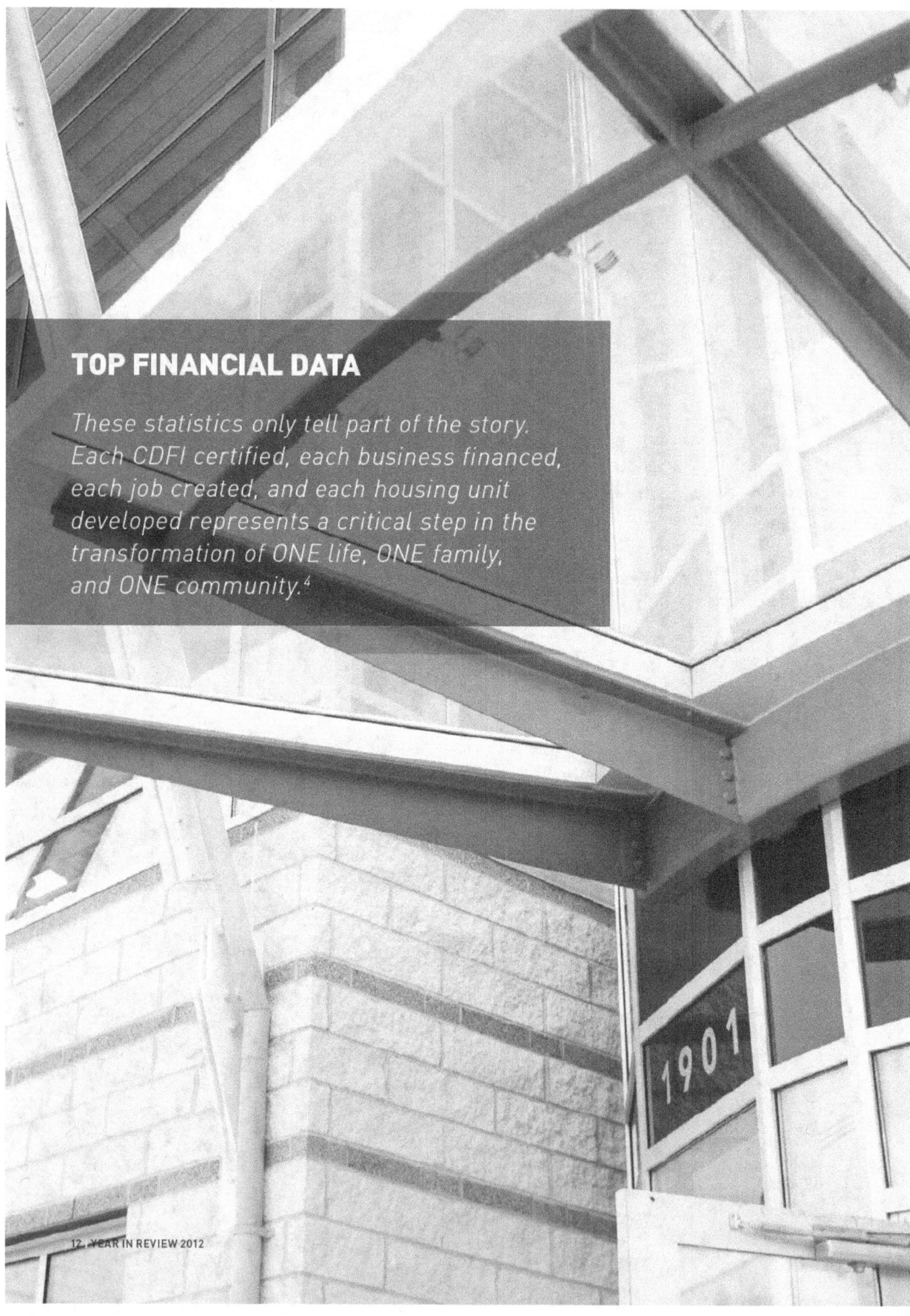

TOP FINANCIAL DATA

These statistics only tell part of the story. Each CDFI certified, each business financed, each job created, and each housing unit developed represents a critical step in the transformation of ONE life, ONE family, and ONE community.[4]

FY 2012 DATA

56
The number of Community Development Financial Institutions certified in FY 2012.

$175 MILLION
The single largest award round for the CDFI Program to date.

$432.4 MILLION
The increase in amount spent on community development projects by BEA Program applicants over their prior year's investment in these types of projects.

$5.5 BILLION
The amount in loans and investments in low-income communities made possible under the New Markets Tax Credit Program, of which 70% were in severely distressed communities.

4,102
The number of businesses financed by CDFI Program awardees.

24,466
The number of affordable housing units financed by CDFI Program awardees.

18.6 MILLION
The amount of square feet of commercial real estate developed from financing from New Markets Tax Credit allocatees. In other words, over 320 football fields worth of commercial real estate.

25,618
The number of jobs created or maintained through CDFI Program awardees.

31,405
The number of jobs created from the funds allocated through the New Markets Tax Credit Program.

Source: CDFI Fund FY 2012 Annual Financial Report.

$1.7 BILLION
The total amount that the CDFI Fund awarded to CDFIs, community development organizations, and financial institutions since its creation in 1994.

$33 BILLION
The total amount that the CDFI Fund awarded in tax credit authority to Community Development Entities through the NMTC Program over nine allocation rounds.

$1.2 BILLION
The total amount the CDFI Program has awarded to organizations since it was launched in 1994.

$336 MILLION
The total amount the BEA Program has awarded to organizations since it was launched in 1994.

70.5 PERCENT
The percentage of NMTC loans and investments made in Severely Distressed Communities.

34,295
The total number of businesses provided with financial counseling and other services by NMTC Program allocatees.

109.3 MILLION
The total amount of square feet of commercial real estate developed from financing from NMTC Program allocatees.

111,277
The total number of jobs created from the funds allocated through the NMTC Program.

1,750
The total number of hours of technical assistance that has been provided to CDFIs since the Capacity Building Initiative was created in 2011.

HISTORICAL DATA

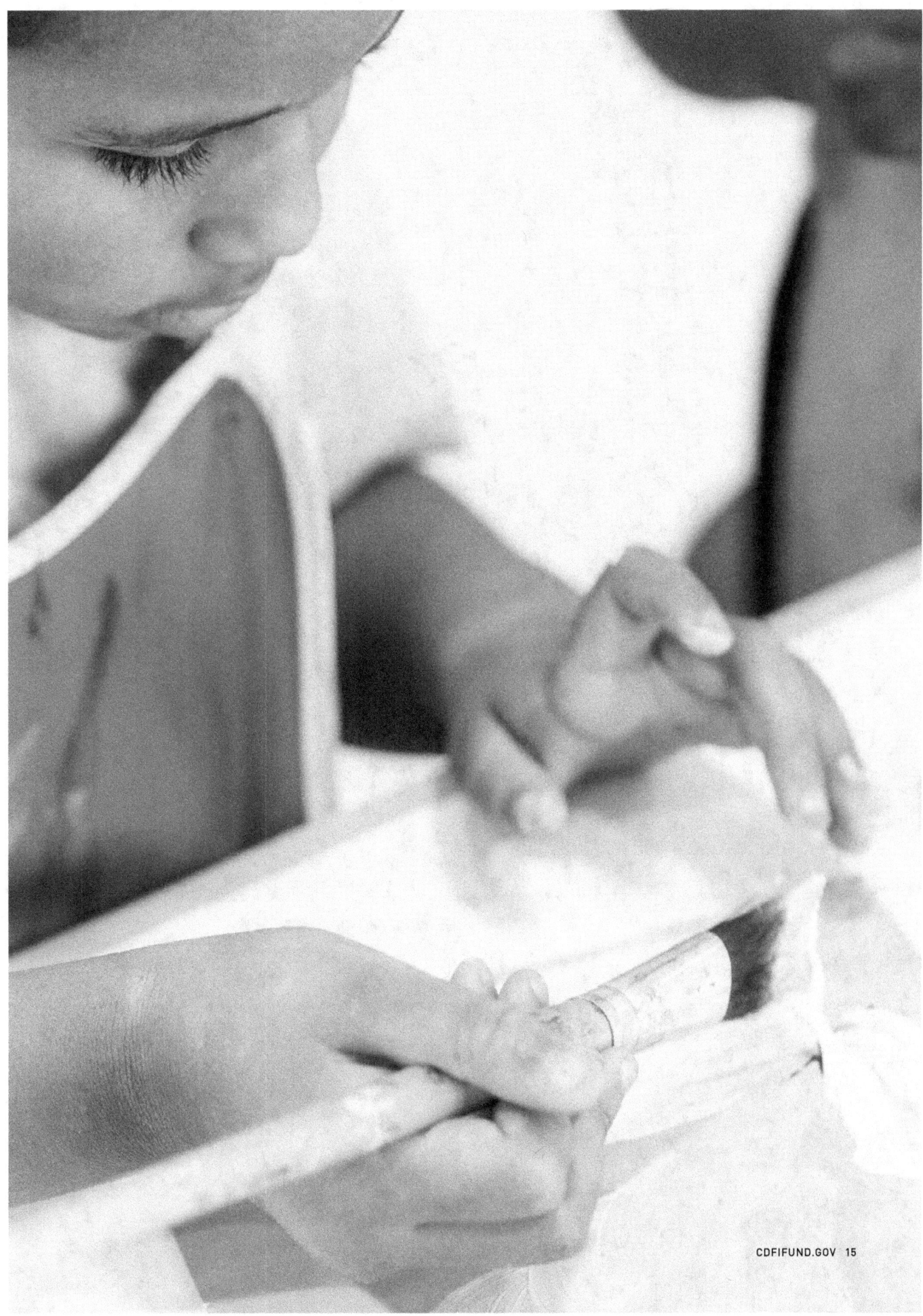

PROGRAM ACHIEVEMENTS

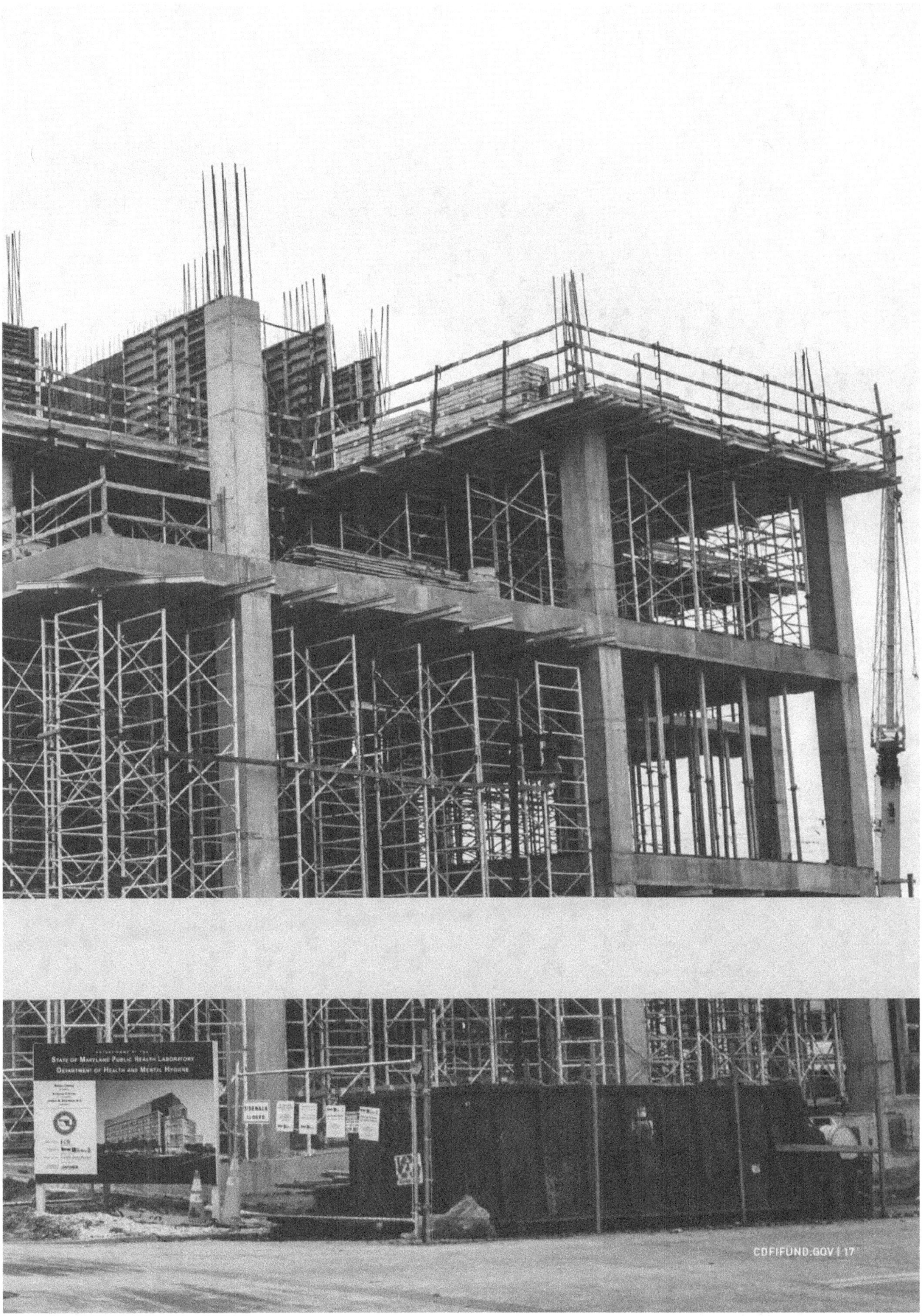
State of Maryland Public Health Laboratory
Department of Health and Mental Hygiene
Sidewalk Closed

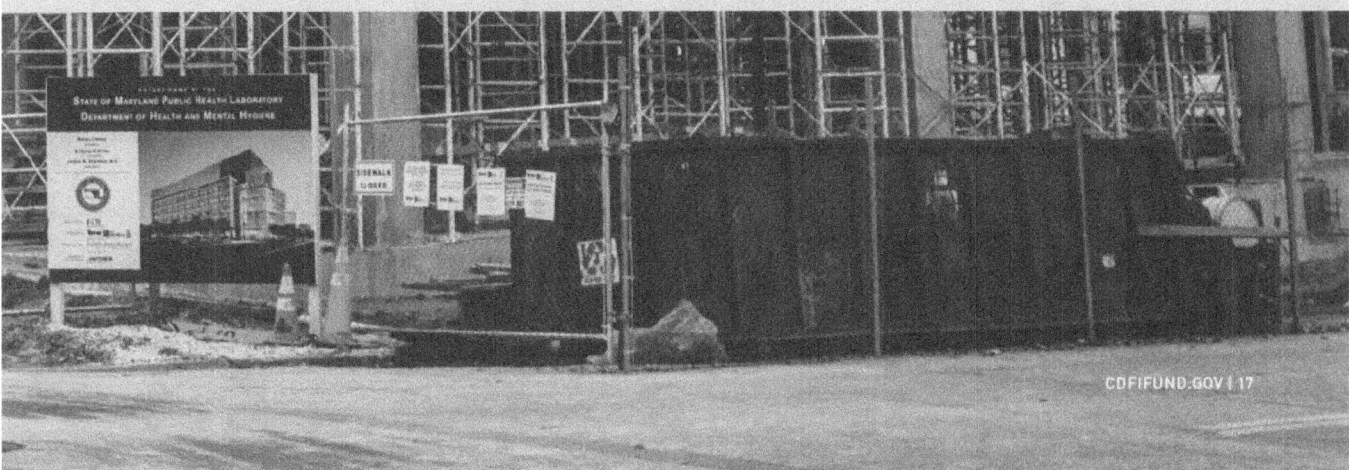

COMMUNITY DEVELOPMENT FINANCIAL INSTITUTIONS PROGRAM

Since the program's inception in 1994, organizations have received nearly **$1.2 billion** in **Financial Assistance** and **Technical Assistance**.

---

www.cdfifund.gov/cdfi

The CDFI Program is the only Federal program dedicated to building and expanding CDFIs which promote economic revitalization in low-income communities.

The CDFI Program invests in and builds the capacity of CDFIs, empowering them to grow, achieve organizational sustainability, and contribute to the revitalization of their communities.

The CDFI Fund uses limited federal resources to invest in communities that lack access to affordable financial products and services.

There are two types of monetary awards given through the CDFI Program: Financial Assistance and Technical Assistance. Community Development Financial Institutions use these funds to:

- Promote economic development by supporting small businesses, creating jobs and developing commercial real estate.

- Develop affordable housing and promote home ownership.

- Provide financial services, including basic banking services, financial literacy programs and alternatives to predatory lending.

The CDFI Program awarded $175.3 million to CDFIs in FY 2012.

Financial Assistance Awards

Financial Assistance Awards are given in the form of investments, loans, deposits and grants to help existing Community Development Financial Institutions.

Any CDFI that receives a Financial Assistance Award must match the amount dollar-for-dollar with non-Federal funds. This empowers CDFIs to leverage outside resources to meet the demand in their economically stressed communities.

TOTAL CDFI PROGRAM AWARDS (IN MILLIONS)[5]

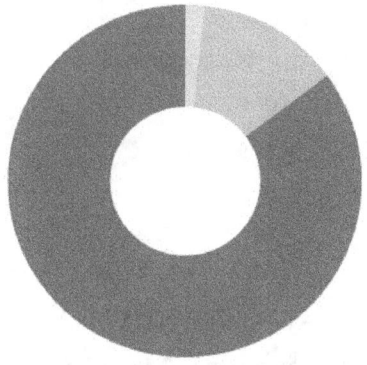

$149.20 Financial Assistance

$23 Healthy Food Financing Initiative

$3 Technical Assistance

[5]Source for Chart: CDFI Fund FY 2012 Annual Financial Report.

In FY 2012, the CDFI Fund received **Financial Assistance applications from 273 community organizations** requesting more than **$367.6 million** in funding.

Through a rigorous selection process, the CDFI Fund awarded a total of **$149.2 million** to **144 organizations** throughout the U.S.

These statistics show the critical need for community investments, loans, deposits and grants. Because there is such high demand for Financial Assistance, the CDFI Fund decided to cap awards at $1.45 million each in 2012. This allows more CDFIs to receive the funding they need to build their communities.

HEALTHY FOOD FINANCING INITIATIVE

In FY 2011, the CDFI Fund coordinated with the Department of Agriculture and the Department of Health and Human Services to launch the Healthy Food Financing Initiative (HFFI). The CDFI Fund's component of the HFFI is administered under the CDFI Program.

The CDFI Fund is taking a holistic approach by providing flexible financial assistance and specialized training and technical assistance to CDFIs that invest in businesses that provide healthy food options. The businesses supported by CDFIs may work on the production, distribution, or retail aspects of the business cycle.

The CDFI Fund awarded more than $23 million in Financial Assistance Awards in FY 2012 to help 12 CDFIs finance healthy food activities.

Technical Assistance Awards

Technical Assistance awards provide grants to build the capacity for both start-up and existing CDFIs. These grants are used for staff salaries, benefits, training, professional services, supplies and equipment. Unlike the Financial Assistance awards, there are no matching requirements for these grants.

The CDFI Fund received **116 Technical Assistance applications** in FY 2012, requesting more than **$11.1 million** in grants.

After the CDFI Fund selection process, **33 organizations** were awarded a total of **$3 million.**

Newly certified CDFIs often use these funds to develop lending policies and procedures or to build staff lending capacity. More established CDFIs tend to use Technical Assistance Awards to develop new products, serve their market in new ways or upgrade computer hardware or software.

Measuring Success

Financial Assistance and Technical Assistance awardees report their annual performance to the CDFI Fund. This helps both local programs and the CDFI Fund measure and track success.

Here is some top performance measures for awardees, based on program activities reported in FY 2011:

ANNUAL PERFORMANCE OF CDFI PROGRAM AWARDEES FOR FY2012

(BASED ON PROGRAM ACTIVITIES REPORTED IN 2011)[6]

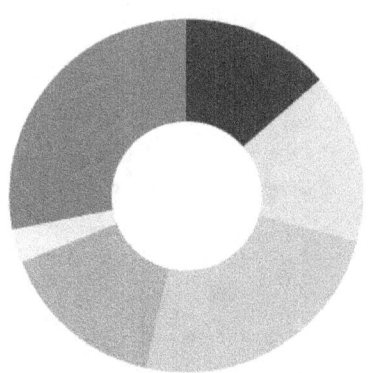

AMOUNT IN MILLIONS

 **$363** Business and Microenterprise

$319 Residential Real Estate Originations

$203 Commercial Real Estate

$198 Home Improvement and Home Purchase

$177 All Other

$39 Consumer

[6]Source: CDFI Fund FY 2012 Annual Financial Report

Lending and Investing Activity	FY 2012
Total Loans/Investments Originated	$1.3 billion
Jobs at End of Reporting Period	25,618 jobs
Affordable Housing Units Financed	24,466 housing units
Businesses Financed	4,102 businesses
Percent of Eligible Areas Served	21.2%

Financial Access and Literacy	FY 2012
Dollars Saved in Individual Development Accounts	$3.2 million
Open Individual Development Accounts	3,216
Individuals Served by Financial Literacy or Other Training	233,100

CAPACITY BUILDING INITIATIVE

www.cdfifund.gov/cbi

The Capacity Building Initiative was developed in the midst of the recent financial crisis, after the CDFI Fund's Community Development Advisory Board determined that there was a pressing need to strengthen and support the overall CDFI industry. The Capacity Building Initiative provides targeted training and technical assistance to both certified and emerging CDFIs nationwide.

Training and technical assistance is provided on-site, in the communities where CDFIs work. Additional online resources and webinars are provided.

At the end of FY 2012, the CDFI Fund was administering four active training series and was in the midst of developing additional training options.

The following four series were completed in FY 2012, although their relevant training materials and external resources are still available as part of the Capacity Building Initiative Resource Bank on the CDFI Fund's website.

These training sessions are developed to target key issues that affect underserved communities, including affordable housing and business lending, portfolio management, risk assessment, foreclosure prevention, general business operations, liquidity and capitalization challenges and more.

FY 2012 TRAINING SERIES :

Foreclosure Solutions
Helped CDFIs build the capacity to operate effective foreclosure intervention programs.

Portfolio Management
Helped CDFIs learn to manage their portfolios and assess and reduce risk.

CDFI Capitalization
Taught CDFIs strategies and techniques for increasing their capitalization and improving liquidity.

Financing Healthy Food Options
Provided CDFIs with tools to eradicate "food deserts" in their target markets.

CAPACITY BUILDING INITIATIVE
RESOURCE BANK

The Capacity Building Initiative Resource Bank is a virtual library of training curricula, webinars, subject-specific reference materials, and third-party expert documents. Accessed through the CDFI Fund's website, the Resource Bank provides varied references on past and current Capacity Building Initiative trainings to allow CDFIs and the general public a one-stop source of information on subjects relevant to the current needs of the CDFI industry.

In addition to the compilation of materials in the Resource Bank, in FY 2012 the CDFI Fund commissioned two specific reports: the "CDFI Industry Analysis: Summary Report," which examines the state of the CDFI industry and its performance through the recent recession; and the "Searching for Markets: The Geography of Inequitable Access to Healthy and Affordable Food" report, which shows that 24.8 million Americans live in areas with limited supermarket access in the continental United States.

The Capacity Building Initiative Resource Bank can be found at **www.cdfifund.gov/cbi**. The research reports can be located in the Resource Bank as well as at **www.cdfifund.gov/research**

Over the two years these four training series — Foreclosure Solutions, Portfolio Management, CDFI Capitalization, and Financing Healthy Food Options — were active:

- 600 individuals received in-person training;

- 1,000 people received virtual training; and

- Over 1,750 hours of technical assistance were provided.

FY 2012 TRAINING SERIES (ACTIVE):

Leadership Journey: Native CDFI Growth and Excellence

Supports the growth and long-term sustainability of Native CDFIs by helping leaders address the critical challenges of their specific organizations.

This training series will close in June, 2013.

Innovations in Small Business Lending

Supports business-oriented CDFIs that are experience in providing loans and services to small and medium-sized enterprises.

This training series will close at the end of FY 2013.

Scaling Up Microfinance

Helps expand the capacity of CDFIs that specialize in microfinance.

This training series will close at the end of calendar year 2014.

Strengthening Small and Emerging CDFIs

Expands the capacity of small and emerging CDFIs through a comprehensive training and technical assistance program.

This training series will close at the end of calendar year 2014.

The CDFI Fund would like to thank the private entities selected to provide the training series: NeighborWorks® America, Opportunity Finance Network, and Deloitte Financial Advisory Services LLP.

HOW DOES THE CAPACITY BUILDING INITIATIVE BENEFIT CDFIS?

CDFIs can access free training workshops, webinars, market research, customized technical assistance, and informational resources to help them develop, diversify, and grow.

NATIVE INITIATIVES

www.cdfifund.gov/native

The Native Initiatives assist entities in overcoming barriers that prevent access to credit, capital, and financial services in Native American, Alaskan Native, and Native Hawaiian communities (Native Communities).

Since the program's inception in 2001, the **number of certified Native CDFIs increased from 7 to over 70**, and Native CDFIs have received over **$81 million** in **Financial Assistance** and **Technical Assistance awards.**

The Native Initiatives' central component is the Native American CDFI Assistance Program (NACA Program), which increases the number and capacity of existing or new CDFIs serving Native Communities. Native CDFIs focus, largely, on two different financial sectors: 1) affordable housing; and 2) economic development.

In FY 2012, the CDFI Fund received **66 NACA eligible applications** requesting a total of **\$20.94 million** for both FA and TA funding. The CDFI Fund was able to provide awards to half of the eligible applications by awarding **33 organizations** a total of **\$11.5 million** for both Financial Assistance and Technical Assistance funding.

TOTAL FA & TA FUNDING

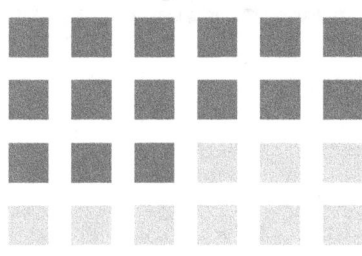

FA - 15 organizations awarded \$9 million

TA - 18 organizations awarded \$2.4 million

ADDITIONAL INITIATIVES

In addition, the Native Initiatives provide training through the Capacity Building Initiative, such as the Leadership Journey: Native CDFI Growth and Excellence series, to support continued growth and long-term sustainability of Native CDFIs. See pages 22-25, the Capacity Building Initiative, for more information.

NEW MARKETS TAX CREDIT PROGRAM

www.cdfifund.gov/nmtc

The New Markets Tax Credit Program (NMTC Program) helps economically distressed communities attract private investment capital by providing investors with a Federal tax credit. Investments made through the NMTC Program are used to finance businesses and real estate projects, breathing new life into neglected, underserved low-income communities.

The NMTC Program permits taxpayers to receive a credit against federal income taxes for making Qualified Equity Investments (QEIs) in designated Community Development Entities (CDEs). The CDEs in turn use the capital raised to make investments in low-income communities. The CDFI Fund is responsible for awarding tax credit allocation authority to CDEs.

Unlike the CDFI Fund's other programs, the NMTC Program operates on a calendar year, not fiscal year, schedule to parallel the tax year. Since the program's inception in 2002:

Demand for NMTC allocation authority has been very high, as 2,388 applicants have requested tax credits supporting a total of more than $229 billion in equity investments.

The CDFI Fund has completed nine allocation rounds and has made 664 awards totaling $33 billion in allocation authority. This $33 billion includes $3 billion in Recovery Act Awards and $1 billion of special allocation authority to be used for the recovery and redevelopment of the Gulf Opportunity Zone.

The CDFI Fund received **282 New Markets Tax Credit** applications in 2012, requesting nearly **$22 billion** in allocation authority.

Upon completing its review process, the CDFI Fund will announce in April 2013 those applicants selected to receive **$3.5 billion in New Markets Tax Credits.**

[7] Source: CDFI Fund FY 2012 Annual Financial Report

[8] Qualified Low-Income Community Investments.

Note: Allocatees report QEI and QLICI activity to the CDFI Funds through the Allocation Tracking System (ATS) and Community Investment Impact System (CIIS). Annual performance data represents the allocatees' CIIS data reported for FY 2012 (program year 2011). Cumulative performance data is based on program activities reported in 2003-2011.

The NMTC Program's innovative approach to using tax credits to promote economic development in low-income communities led to its recognition as a "Bright Idea in Government" by Harvard University's Ash Center for Democratic Governance and Innovation at the John F. Kennedy School of Government.

CUMULATIVE AND ANNUAL PERFORMANCE OF NMTC PROGRAM ALLOCATEES[7]

Lending and Investing Activity	FY 2012	Cumulative
Total QLICI[8]	$5.5 billion	$26.4 billion
Number of QLICI	1,278 QLICIs	6,814 QLICIs
Percent of Loans/Investments in Severely Distressed Communities	70.6%	70.5%
Jobs at End of Reporting Period	31,405 jobs	111,277 jobs
Projected Construction Jobs	52,448 jobs	247,555 jobs
Affordable Housing Units Financed	2,967 housing units	7,488 housing units
Sq. Ft. of Commercial Real Estate	18.6 million sq. ft.	109.3 million sq. ft.
Businesses Financed	578 businesses	1,781 businesses

Financial Counseling and Other Services	FY 2012	Cumulative
Total Investments	$856,979	$33.1 million
Businesses Served	8,323 businesses	34,295 businesses

BANK ENTERPRISE AWARD PROGRAM

www.cdfifund.gov/bea

The Bank Enterprise Award Program (BEA Program) awards FDIC-insured depository institutions for making investments in the most distressed communities throughout the nation.

Since the program's inception in 1994, the BEA Program has awarded grants totaling approximately **$376 million.**

BEA PROGRAM

BEA Program awardees are recognized for their investment in CDFIs and for their work in communities where 30% of the population lives at or below the national poverty level and unemployment is at least 1.5 times the national average. Organizations that receive awards must then reinvest that money back into distressed communities.

FY 2012 BEA Program Awards

In FY 2012, the CDFI Fund provided nearly **$18 million** in BEA Program awards to **59 organizations** headquartered in 18 states and the District of Columbia.

FY 2012 BEA COMMUNITY IMPACT

FY 2012 BEA Program awardees increased their qualified community development activities by over $409.9 million, including:

$5.5 MILLION
Increase in the provision of financial services in distressed communities

$21.1 MILLION
Increase in loans, deposits, and technical assistance to CDFIs

$383.3 MILLION
Increase in loans and investments in distressed communities

$409.9 MILLION
FY 2012 BEA community impact

CDFI BOND GUARANTEE PROGRAM

www.cdfifund.gov/bond

The CDFI Bond Guarantee Program was authorized through the Small Business Jobs Act of 2010, and provides CDFIs access to a significant source of capital. By providing guarantees of bonds issued by certain qualified bond issuers, the CDFI Bond Guarantee Program injects new and substantial capital into our nation's most distressed communities.

CDFIs can gain from the potential scale of the CDFI Bond Guarantee Program, which offers long-term credit at below-market interest rates. Administered by the CDFI Fund, the program is a groundbreaking effort to accelerate community economic revitalization.

Through the CDFI Bond Guarantee Program, qualified entities (CDFIs or their designees) will issue bonds that are guaranteed by the Federal government and use the bond proceeds to extend or refinance credit to the broader CDFI industry for community development purposes. CDFIs use these bonds to make investments in underserved communities.

The bonds or notes will support CDFI lending and investment by providing a source of long-term capital to CDFIs. The Treasury may guarantee up to 10 bonds per year, each at a minimum of $100 million, and the total of all bonds cannot exceed $1 billion per year.

Unlike other CDFI Fund programs, the CDFI Bond Guarantee Program is a "self-pay" initiative. CDFIs are taking on a debt obligation that must be repaid. This allows for flexibility for CDFIs in their spending, while balancing overall lending risk for the CDFI Fund.

CDFIs can use these loans for a number of financial activities, such as financing low-income housing, or supporting small businesses that provide jobs for low-income people or are owned by low-income people.

Pending Congressional authority, the CDFI Fund anticipates that the first bond issuance will occur in 2013.

ADMINISTRATIVE
ACHIEVEMENTS

Behind the Scenes
at the
CDFI FUND

At the close of FY 2012, the CDFI Fund had 67 employees working in program administration, compliance and certification activities, legal services, legislative affairs, external outreach and training, information technology, human resources, and administrative support.

Moving Office Location

During FY 2012, the CDFI Fund relocated their office from 601 13th Street NW, Washington, D.C. to 1801 L Street NW, Washington, D.C. as a means to cut back on office building expenses.

$405,097

The annual cost avoidance for the CDFI Fund with the new office location.

$4.05 MIL

The projected cost avoidance over the next decade for the CDFI Fund.

Incorporating New IT Services

The CDFI Fund is leveraging the Alcohol and Tobacco Tax and Trade Bureau (TTB), another bureau within Treasury for its Information Technology (IT) resources and services (i.e., telecommunications, data center and desktop management) to avoid a costly refresh of its IT equipment.

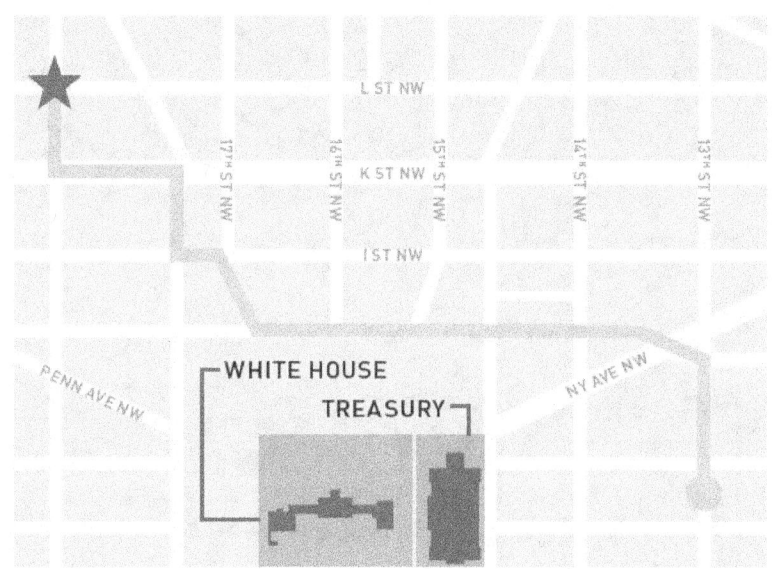

The CDFI Fund's technology service was outdated and the aging equipment was prone to failures, making it difficult to support more modern technologies. After examining the IT refresh plan, TTB offered to host the CDFI Fund on their infrastructure to avoid creating a completely new infrastructure for the CDFI Fund and to avoid having to acquire new equipment.

$3.5 MIL

The cost avoidance over three years by collaborating with TTB.

The CDFI Fund was also able to decommission both its onsite and disaster recovery data centers as part of this transition. Decommissioning these two data centers has enabled Treasury to reduce the overall energy and real estate footprint of its data centers while increasing both security and efficiency.

Strengthening Compliance and Certification Management

The CDFI Fund aspires to ensure that its compliance management function is a robust effort that:

- Identifies all instances of non-compliance with assistance and allocation agreements on a timely basis;

- Pursues quick corrective actions in response to instances of non-compliance; and

- Identifies existing awardees and allocatees whose overall financial health presents a significant risk for continued investment of public funds and pursues appropriate actions in response to findings.

In FY 2012, CDFI Fund continued its efforts to strengthen the oversight of award recipients by allocating five new staff positions to the Certification, Compliance Monitoring, and Evaluation business unit, representing an increase in compliance management staffing of nearly 50 percent over FY 2011 staffing levels.

The CDFI Fund has also developed a performance metrics baseline for the compliance portfolio, and has reviewed its business processes related to compliance management to increase operational efficiency. These initiatives support the CDFI Fund's strategic goal of aligning resources and human capital management to maximize performance, efficiency, and program results.

Financial Strategy and Research

The CDFI Fund's Office of Financial Strategy and Research (FS&R) evaluates the impact of the CDFI Fund's programs on communities across the country through data collection and analysis of the activities of awardees and allocatees.

In FY 2012, the FS&R team launched the CDFI Program Evaluation Project to determine how and to what extent the program's investments in CDFIs have benefited and contributed to the development of underserved communities. The evaluation will assess industry-wide performance benchmarks for awardees and compare these outcomes with appropriate peer groups of non-awardee CDFIs (both certified CDFIs and non-certified CDFIs) to better gauge the relative impact of the program on financial performance, risk, and social impacts.

The CDFI Fund has already released transaction-level public data of CDFI Program activities covering the 2004-2010 time period. The release of the data in 2012 marked the first time that transaction-level data was made available to the public, enabling researchers to look at the location, structure, and performance of over 400,000 individual loans and investments made by 239 CDFIs. The data was reported by CDFIs through the Community Investment Impact System. New Markets Tax Credit transactional data from 2003-2010 was also released in 2012.

The FS&R team has also been developing new census-tract program eligibility data for the CDFI Fund's programs based upon the 5-year 2006-2010 American Community Survey. The New Markets Tax Credit Program eligibility was deployed in May 2012, the CDFI Program and NACA Program eligibility in February 2013, and the BEA Program eligibility is expected later in 2013.

Two significant research reports were produced in 2012: the *CDFI Industry Analysis: Summary Report and Searching for Markets: The Geography of Inequitable Access to Healthy and Affordable Food.* These reports were produced as industry resources for the CDFI Fund's Capacity Building Initiative.

The CDFI Industry Analysis: Summary Report examines the state of the CDFI industry and its performance through the recent recession. The report explores a variety of important issues to help CDFIs serve more people, access more funds, and increase their impact.

Searching for Markets: The Geography of Inequitable Access to Healthy and Affordable Food, showed that 24.8 million Americans live in areas with limited supermarket access in the continental United States. This study will help CDFIs target their resources in areas of highest need.

Outreach and Public Engagement

In order to garner interest and promote application for various program awards, the staff, including the Director, partakes in diverse outreach and public engagement efforts. During FY 2012, from October 1, 2011 to September 30, 2012, the CDFI Fund staff:

- Created 50 unique press releases for major announcements or events;

- Participated in over 70 conferences, workshops, roundtables, webinars, and conference calls; and

- Wrote 12 keynote speeches for the Director to use at the major conferences listed below.

2011 New Markets Tax Credit Coalition Annual Conference

2012 National Interagency Community Reinvestment Conference

Association for Enterprise Opportunity National Conference

National Bankers Association 84th Annual Convention

Opportunity Finance Network Conference - Eighth Annual Native Gathering

Opportunity Finance Network Conference - General Session

Reznick Group's 2012 New Markets Tax Credit Summit

SRI in the Rockies

Sustainable Finance Panel at the Clinton Global Initiative America

The CDFI Coalition's 2012 CDFI Institute

The National Community Investment Fund's Annual Development Banking Conference

The National Federation of Community Development Credit Unions' 38th Annual Conference on Serving the Underserved

Collaborations with Government Partners

In FY 2012, the CDFI Fund actively worked to collaborate with several government partners on promising initiatives and programs. Now more than ever, these kinds of partnerships are critical to the development of the CDFI industry. In the wake of the financial crisis and the many challenges it has created, working together by pooling the expertise, creativity, and resources of diverse agencies, will enable our industry to reach new levels of success.

THE HEALTHY FOOD FINANCING INITIATIVE
CDFI FUND & HHS & USDA

See pages 18-21, the CDFI Program, for more information.

THE COMMUNITY ADVANTAGE PROGRAM
CDFI FUND & SBA

In an effort to expand access to capital for small businesses and entrepreneurs in underserved communities across the nation, SBA created a new loan initiative, Community Advantage. The pilot program will increase the number of lower-dollar loans into these underserved communities by allowing CDFI loan funds, and other mission-focused lenders, to originate SBA 7(a) loans up to $250,000.

THE BORDER COMMUNITY CAPITAL INITIATIVE (BORDER INITIATIVE)
CDFI FUND & HUD & SBA

The Border Initiative is a collaboration designed to increase access to capital by helping to create jobs and expand opportunities in the U.S./Mexico border region (colonias), which includes some of the poorest communities in the country. The three agencies signed a Memorandum of Understanding that will offer up to $200,000 to nonprofit and/or tribal financial institutions serving colonias for direct investment and technical assistance focusing on affordable housing, small businesses, and community facilities.

CDFI FUND FY2013 STRATEGIC PRIORITIES

As you take a look back at the remarkable achievements the CDFI Fund has accomplished in FY 2012, let us remind you that the CDFI Fund is constantly striving to better the organization and create new strategic goals for the upcoming years.

Compliance
Building a stronger compliance infrastructure to review and assess CDFI and CDE adherence with program requirements.

Certification
Recertifying CDFIs to ensure institutions maintain certification status while upholding the CDFI brand.

CDFI Support
Continuing to build the capacity of CDFIs while supporting the changing role of CDFIs in a recovering economy.

Operations
Developing and reevaluating policies and processes to streamline operations and improve administrative efficiency and efficacy.

Relationships
Fostering intergovernmental, non-profit and private partnerships to leverage resources for CDFIs.

Additional Goals

Employee Development: Training and development to maintain and enhance skills, experience, and abilities.

Program Administration: Innovative approaches to strengthen programs.

Photo Credits

Capital Area Food Bank
4900 Puerto Rico Avenue, NE,
Washington, DC 20017

City First Bank of DC
1432 U Street, NW,
Washington, DC 20009

**East Baltimore
Development, Inc.**
1731 East Chase Street,
Baltimore MD 21213

Heller's Bakery
3221 Mt. Pleasant Street, NW,
Washington, DC 20010

Rhode Island Stations
919 Rhode Island Avenue, NE,
Washington, DC 20018

**THEARC –
The Town Hall Education
Arts Recreation Campus**
1901 Mississippi Avenue, SE
Washington, DC 20020

CDFI FUND

1801 L STREET NW
6TH FLOOR
WASHINGTON, DC 20220

CDFIFUND.GOV